THE BLUEST EYE

by
Toni Morrison

Teacher Guide

Written by
Pat Watson

> **Note**
> The Plume paperback edition of the book, published by the Penguin Group, ©1970, Afterword ©1993, was used to prepare this guide. The page references may differ in other editions.
>
> **Please note:** This novel deals with sensitive, mature issues. Parts may contain profanity, sexual references, and/or descriptions of violence. Please assess the appropriateness of this book for the age level and maturity of your students prior to reading it with your class.

ISBN 1-58130-708-X

Copyright infringement is a violation of Federal Law.

© 2001, 2004 by Novel Units, Inc., Bulverde, Texas. All rights reserved. No part of this publication may be reproduced, translated, stored in a retrieval system, or transmitted in any way or by any means (electronic, mechanical, photocopying, recording, or otherwise) without prior written permission from Novel Units, Inc.

Photocopying of student worksheets by a classroom teacher at a non-profit school who has purchased this publication for his/her own class is permissible. Reproduction of any part of this publication for an entire school or for a school system, by for-profit institutions and tutoring centers, or for commercial sale is strictly prohibited.

Novel Units is a registered trademark of Novel Units, Inc.

Printed in the United States of America.

To order, contact your local school supply store, or—

Novel Units, Inc.
P.O. Box 433
Bulverde, TX 78163-0433

Web site: www.educyberstor.com

Table of Contents

Summary 3

About the Author 5

Initiating Activities 6

Nine Sections 13
    Each section contains: Summary, Vocabulary,
    Discussion Questions, and Supplementary Activities

Post-reading Discussion Questions 26

Post-reading Extension Activities 28

Assessment 29

Glossary 30

Skills and Strategies

Thinking
Research, compare/contrast, analysis

Vocabulary
Target words, definitions, application

Listening/Speaking
Discussion, oral presentation

Comprehension
Predictions, cause/effect, current events

Literary Elements
Characterization, personification, simile, metaphor, allusion, theme, symbolism, universality

Writing
Poems, response, dictionary, critique, personal, advertisements

Across the Curriculum
Art—collage, drawing, montage; Drama—acting, script; Music—ballad

Genre: fiction

Setting: Lorain, Ohio, early 1940s

Point of View: first-person and third-person omniscient

Themes: self-hatred, rejection, racism, survival

Conflict: self vs. self; family conflict; race vs. race

Subject Material: adolescence, self-image, sexuality, incest, family relationships, mental illness

Style: passages shift between narrative and the third-person omniscient voice, including stream of consciousness

Tone: pessimistic, hopeless

Date of first publication: 1970

Summary

Pecola Breedlove, an eleven-year-old black girl, grows up in the hopelessness of a dysfunctional family and the rejection of white people and prosperous black families. She prays for blue eyes, believing this will make her loved and accepted. Pecola is raped and impregnated by her father, but the baby dies when it is born too soon. The trauma of her life and the manipulation of a self-proclaimed psychic drive her into madness.

Claudia MacTeer relates the first-person narrative sections and the omniscient voice provides information with which Claudia is not familiar. Stream-of-consciousness segments provide additional information through fragmented memories.

Characters

The Breedlove Family
Pecola: protagonist; poor, considered ugly, rejected by almost everyone in her life; convinced that only those with blue eyes are accepted and loved; is raped and impregnated by her father; after the rape, invents an imaginary friend with whom she converses

Pauline: wife and mother; has a lame foot; harsh and abusive toward her family; an "ideal" employee, kind and considerate to the Fisher family, for whom she works; vindictively religious, develops a "martyr" image

Cholly: husband and father; slothful, abusive alcoholic; abandoned as a child by his parents; raised by his great aunt; rapes his daughter; dies in the workhouse

Sammy: teenage son and brother; unhappy; often gets in trouble and runs away from home

Great Aunt Jimmy: elderly woman who takes Cholly to raise after his mother abandons him; dies when Cholly is a teenager

Samson Fuller: presumably Cholly's father; humiliates Cholly in their only encounter

The MacTeer Family
Claudia: nine-year-old first-person narrator of first segment of each unit; bright, caring, sensitive; rejects idea of "white" standards of beauty

Frieda: Claudia's ten-year-old sister; strong, bold; concerned about Pecola

Mrs. MacTeer: the girls' mother; protective; loving but not indulgent; authoritative

Mr. MacTeer: the girls' father; appears harsh at times but is a loving, concerned parent

Others (in order of appearance)
Rosemary: girl who lives next door to the MacTeers; tattletale

Mr. Henry: the MacTeers' boarder; can be charming but has lewd tendencies; makes sexual advances toward Frieda

Mr. Yacobowski: store owner who treats Pecola with contempt

China, Poland, Marie (also called the Maginot Line): three prostitutes who live in a room above the Breedloves; treat Pecola kindly; names symbolic, referring to countries threatened by invasion or already occupied by fascist armies during World War II

Maureen Peal: new student; mulatto, more affluent than other children; haughty; treats Pecola kindly at first but turns against her

Geraldine: comfortably wealthy black woman; concerned with respectability; disdainful of poor blacks; incapable of maternal love but consumed with love for her cat

Louis, Jr.: Geraldine's son; devious; kills a cat, then blames Pecola, causing his mother to retaliate against her

Blue Jack: father figure in Cholly's childhood

M'Dear: sensible, authoritative old woman who gives Aunt Jimmy medical advice

Darlene: teenage girl with whom Cholly is involved sexually when white men humiliate him

Soaphead Church (Elihue Micah Whitcomb): man from the West Indies of mixed black and white parentage; has pedophiliac tendencies toward little girls; town psychic whose "magic" is the last step in Pecola's descent into insanity

Bertha Reese: old woman from whom Soaphead rents his room

About the Author

Personal Information

Toni Morrison, whose birth name is Chloe Anthony Wofford, was born in 1931 in Lorain, Ohio. She is the second of four children born to George and Ramah Wofford. She married Harold Morrison in 1958; they were divorced in 1964. She has two children, Harold Ford and Slade Kevin. She graduated from Lorain High School in 1949 and earned a Bachelor of Arts in English from Howard University in 1953 and a Master of Arts from Cornell University in 1955. She is also the trustee of the National Humanities Center and co-chairs the Schomburg Commission for the Preservation of Black Culture. Memberships include American Academy and Institute of Arts and Letters, American Academy of Arts and Sciences, National Council on the Arts, Authors Guild, Authors League of America, and Alpha Kappa Alpha Sorority.

Career

Morrison was an instructor in English at Texas Southern University in Houston, Texas (1955-57) and at Howard University in Washington, D.C. (1957-64). She was the senior editor at Random House from 1965-1985. In addition, she served as associate professor of English at State University of New York at Purchase (1971-72), as the Albert Schweitzer Chair in the Humanities at State University of New York at Albany (1984-89), and as the Robert F. Goheen Professor in the Council of the Humanities at Princeton University (1989-). She began her literary career with her first novel, *The Bluest Eye*, published in 1970. Other works include the novels *Sula* (1973), *Song of Solomon* (1977), *Tar Baby* (1981), *Beloved* (1987), *Jazz* (1992), *Paradise* (1998); a play, *Dreaming Emmett* (1986), and a collection of essays, *Playing in the Dark: Whiteness and the Literary Imagination* (1992).

Honors

Morrison received the Nobel prize for Literature in 1993. Other honors include: National Book Award nomination and Ohioana Book Award for *Sula* (1975); National Book Critics Circle Award and American Academy and Institute of Arts and Letters Award for *Song of Solomon* (1977); New York State Governor's Arts Award (1986), first recipient of the Washington College Literary award, National Book Award nomination (1987), National Book Critics Circle Award nomination (1987), Pulitzer Prize for fiction (1988) and Robert F. Kennedy Award (1988) for *Beloved*.

Source: http://www.cs.utexas.edu/users/lakhia/Morrison/biograph.html

Initiating Activities

Use one or more of the following to introduce the novel.

1. Have students rate the following needs, with number 1 being the most crucial to the development of self-esteem in children: praise; physical affection; encouragement in development of talents; quality time with parent(s); freedom to fail, with encouragement to try again; valuing a child's opinion; money; listening to a child's concerns; consistent, loving discipline; unconditional love; allowing child to make decisions. This can be a classroom or individual project.

2. Have students rate the following detriments to the development of a child's self-esteem, with number 1 being the most damaging: abuse; ridicule; criticism; comparison with siblings or peers; degrading comments such as "stupid," "messy," or "dumb"; failure to give child time and attention; degrading child in front of peers or teachers; not enough affection; verbal put-downs; not allowing child to make decisions; strife between parents.

3. Place the term "self-hatred" on the overhead transparency. Brainstorm with students: root causes, associated emotions, results, solutions.

4. Bring a copy of a "Dick and Jane" primer to class. Read portions and discuss the stereotypes: race, family structure, physical attributes, house.

5. Read aloud Maya Angelou's poem, "Caged Bird." Discuss what it means to be caged in circumstances or memories. Introduce the character of Pecola Breedlove as one of those "caged birds."

Character Chart

Directions: Choose four characters from the novel and write their names in the blank boxes across the top of the chart. In the boxes across from each of the feelings, describe an incident or time in the book when each character experienced that feeling. You may use "not applicable" if you cannot find an example.

Frustration				
Anger				
Fear				
Humiliation				
Relief				

Feelings

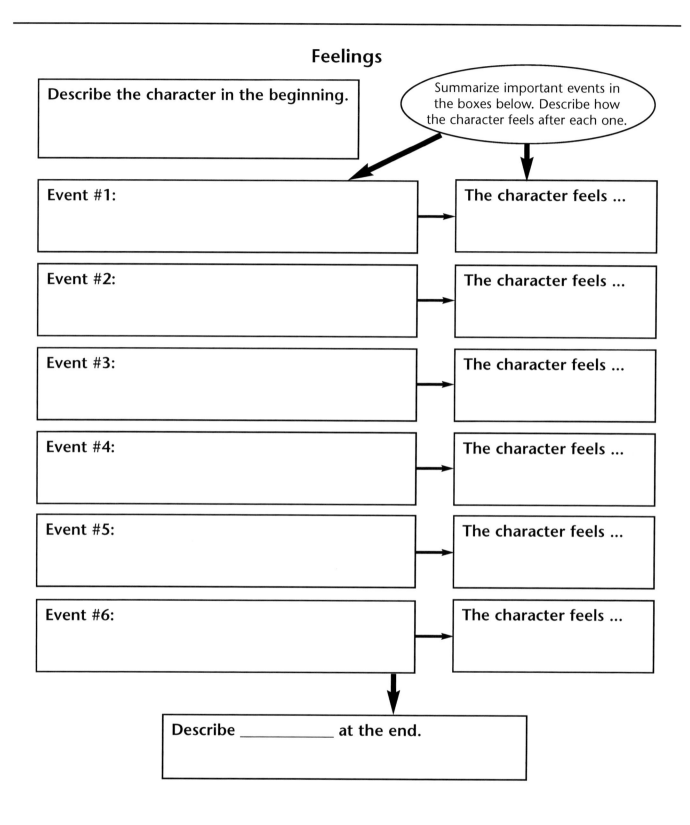

Sociogram

Directions: Complete the sociogram below by adding major and minor characters to the blank ovals. On the arrows, write a word or words to describe the relationship between Pecola and that character. Remember, relationships go both ways, so each line requires a descriptive word. Find examples from the text to justify your answers and refer to page numbers.

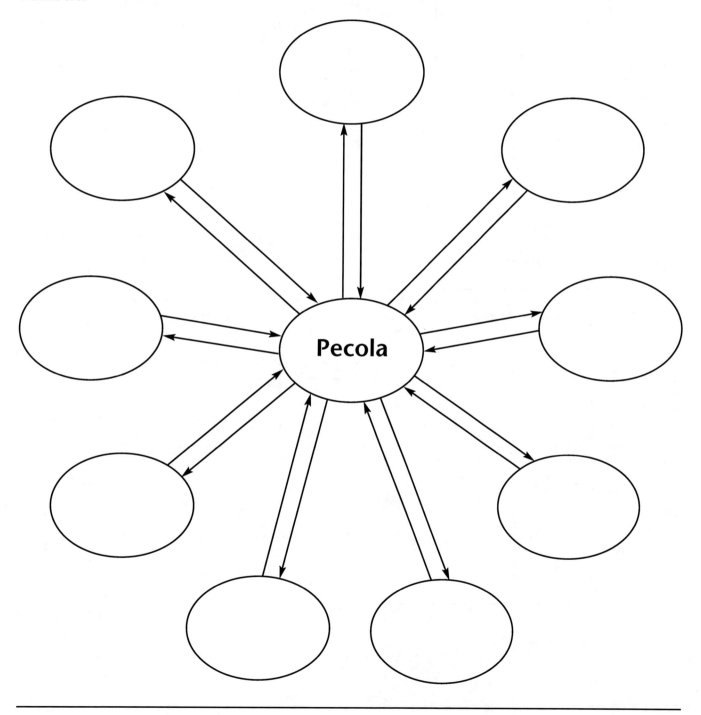

Character Attribute Blocks

Directions: Select a character from the book to tell about using the blocks below.

	Who is the character?

What did the character do?	*Why did s/he do it?*

Why is the character's name well chosen?	*What is the nature of this character's actions?* (reactive, active, important, consequential, secondary)	*What is the significance of the book's time and place to the character?*

What is unusual or important about the character?	*How does the character change in the story?*	*Does the character remind you of another character from another book? Who?*	*Do you know anyone similar to this character?*

Story Map

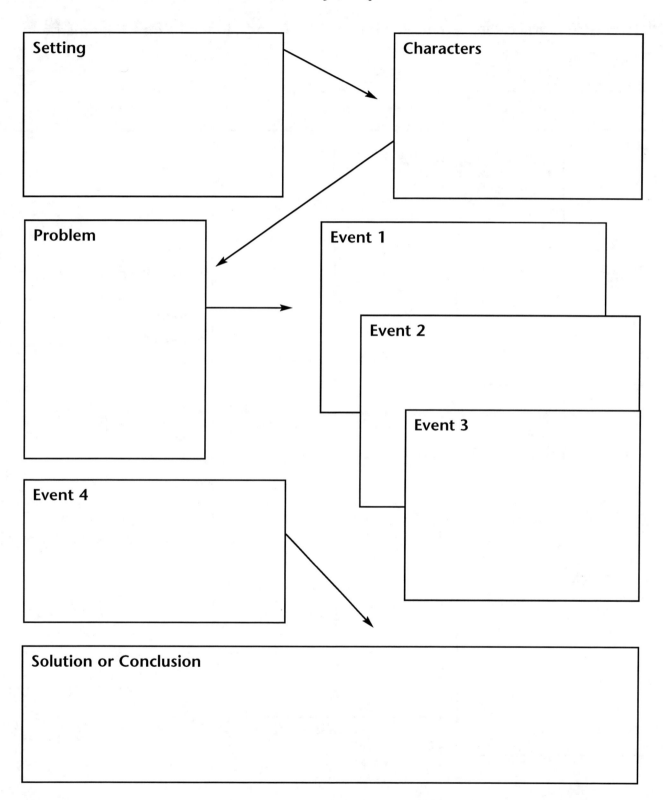

Novel Web Diagram

Directions: The oval is the place for the book's title. Then fill in the boxes to summarize the story.

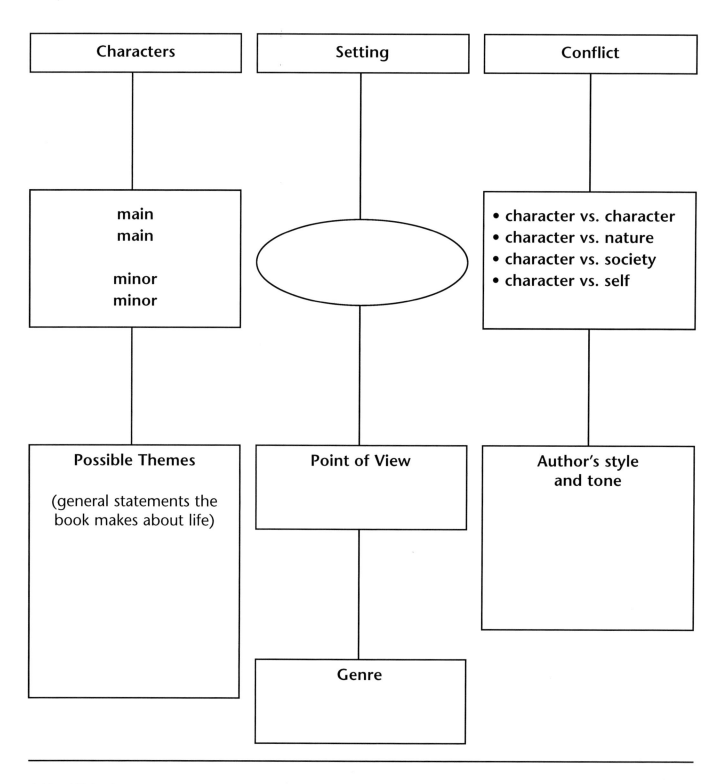

Autumn

Preface–page 32 (primarily first-person)

The preface introduces two ideas: a selection from a "Dick and Jane" primer, which will be used throughout the book to show the decline of Pecola Breedlove's life, and Pecola's impregnation by her own father. Claudia MacTeer, the narrator, reveals that Pecola comes to stay for a few days with the MacTeer family because her father is in jail for setting their house on fire. Pecola begins her menstrual cycle while at the MacTeer's, introducing Claudia and her sister Frieda to the process of maturation.

Vocabulary

melancholy (preface) senile (14) peripheral (17) plaintive (21)
acridness (22) pristine (23) sadism (23) soliloquies (24)
chagrined (24) verification (31)

Discussion Questions

1. Read aloud and analyze the preface. Discuss the selection from the "Dick and Jane" primer and the importance of the portion beginning, "Quiet as it's kept there were no marigolds in the fall of 1941." Note the analogy between the marigold seeds and Cholly's seed. *(The "Dick and Jane" primer presents a perfect family doing exactly the right things, in contrast to the Breedlove family, an imperfect family doing all the wrong things. Claudia reveals a troubling secret. Cholly Breedlove impregnates his daughter, Pecola, because of his lust and despair. The MacTeer sisters believe that, by planting the marigold seeds, they can ensure that Pecola's baby will live. Only in retrospect do the sisters realize it is not their fault that the marigolds do not grow and that the baby dies. The analogy: the sisters drop their seeds in a little plot of black dirt; Pecola's father drops his seeds in his own plot of black dirt. Just as the marigold seeds shrivel and die, so does Pecola's baby. Preface)*

2. Analyze why the words begin to run together in the "Dick and Jane" section. *(Responses will vary. Note this gibberish pattern used to identify the third-person sections, indicating the invalidity of the "perfect family" and the increasing intensity of an out-of-control family [the Breedloves] and Pecola's descent into insanity. Preface)*

3. Discuss Claudia's portrayal of her home and what this reveals about her family. *(Their house is old and drafty, the family is poor, they live economically, and they take in a boarder to help ease financial strain. Their mother's word is law, and, primarily, the children are to fit the cliché of being "seen and not heard." Although their mother speaks brusquely, she shows deep love and concern for Claudia and her sister Frieda. Claudia realizes, as an adult, how much love existed in their home. Although Mrs. MacTeer complains about the amount of food Pecola consumes, she reacts with understanding and compassion when Pecola begins her menstrual cycle. pp. 9-15, 23-25, 31-32)*

4. Discuss why Pecola comes to stay with the MacTeer family and examine what this reveals about her family. *(She comes as a welfare case who has no place to go. She brings nothing with her. Cholly Breedlove, her father, has set their house on fire, hit his wife in the head, and forced his family "outdoors." Cholly is in jail, Mrs. Breedlove is staying with the family for whom she works,*

and Pecola and her brother Sammy are staying with different families. The community considers Cholly to be a "dog." pp. 16-19)

5. Analyze Claudia's reaction to blue-eyed, white baby dolls. *(Claudia, a black child, hates the white dolls and wants to dismember them. Finding them uncomfortable to sleep with and hating their appearance, she breaks off their fingers, loosens their hair, removes their eyes, etc. This hatred extends to little white girls and leads her to despise anything connected with Shirley Temple, who reminds her of the dolls. Claudia's hatred is indicative of her confusion over people's delighted responses to white children but never to her. pp. 19-23)*

6. Examine the relationship between Pecola and the MacTeer sisters. Discuss the universality of the girls' reaction to Pecola's first menstrual period. *(Pecola is complaisant, and the girls get along well. The sisters enjoy having Pecola with them and want her to feel welcome. Pecola is frightened when she begins her menstrual period. Frieda understands what is happening, and the girls attempt to take care of her until their neighbor Rosemary sees them and tells their mother; universality: they realize the importance of such a big event and discuss the possibility of having a baby, showing their partial understanding of sex and maturity. pp. 18-19, 27-32)*

Supplementary Activities

1. Refer to home remedies Mrs. MacTeer uses (pp. 10-11). Have students ask parents or grandparents about early home remedies and present their findings to the class.

2. Have students analyze the metaphor comparing the lives of the black people with a garment: "Being a minority in both caste and class, we moved about anyway on the hem of life, struggling to consolidate our weaknesses and hang on, or to creep singly up into the major folds of the garment" (p. 17).

3. Note the literary devices: **Similes**—nuns go by as quiet as lust (p. 9); it (Claudia's vomit) moves like the insides of an uncooked egg (p. 11); love, thick and dark as Alaga syrup (p. 12); their conversation is like a gently wicked dance...with laughter like the throb of a heart made of jelly (p. 15); propertied black people...like frenzied, desperate birds (p. 18); pearly teeth stuck like two piano keys between red bowline lips (p. 21); cry sounded like bleat of a dying lamb (p. 21); Saturdays sat on my head like a coal scuttle (p. 26) **Metaphor**—Cholly: dog, snake (p. 18) **Allusions**—movie stars Greta Garbo, Ginger Rogers (p. 16), Shirley Temple (p. 19); references to time period: Henry Ford, Roosevelt, CCC camps (p. 25)

Pages 33–58 (third-person omniscient)

Note the phrases from the Dick and Jane reader at the beginning of each third-person section. Relate this "gibberish" to the ensuing section.

This section portrays the bleakness of the Breedloves' home in the front of an abandoned store, their poverty, and their dysfunctional family life. The family is black and believe themselves to be ugly. The parents fight violently, Pecola endures, and her brother, Sammy, runs away or joins the fracas. Pecola prays for blue eyes, believing they will make her beautiful and loved. She finds refuge with the three prostitutes who live above the storefront.

Vocabulary

foists (33)	furtiveness (36)	malaise (37)	dissipation (38)
emasculations (42)	tacitly (43)	inexplicable (50)	petulant (50)
epithets (51)	covert (56)		

Discussion Questions

1. Analyze how the abandoned store symbolizes the Breedloves' lives and how each of the family members reacts to his or her life. *(Both their home and their lives are decaying and hopeless. Their residence in the storefront is nondescript and furnished with characterless relics, symbolizing the bleakness, ugliness, and unhappiness of their lives. They are poor and black, and they believe they are ugly. Cholly, the father, drinks to escape and Mrs. Breedlove has developed a martyr image. They fight violently. Sammy causes pain to others and often runs away from home, and Pecola hides behind a "mask" of endurance. Their lives symbolize the hopelessness of their poverty. pp. 34-44)*

2. Examine the marriage of Cholly and Mrs. Breedlove and their mutual need. *(Their marriage has evolved into quarrels that give substance to the bleakness of their lives. Cholly's drinking and orneriness provide the stimulus they both need to make their lives tolerable. Mrs. Breedlove, the martyr, considers Cholly beyond redemption and herself God's means of vengeance. In her eyes, the meaner he becomes, the more saintly she becomes. Cholly needs her, taking out his self-hatred on her. Yet, their fights parallel the intensity of their lovemaking. pp. 40-43)*

3. Analyze Pecola's reaction to the violence in her home. Discuss the universality of the self-blame of children of violent, dysfunctional parents. *(She becomes physically ill and prays that God will make her disappear. She is able to will herself mentally to fade away but can never get her eyes to disappear. The fights intensify her feelings of ugliness. She believes that, if she had blue eyes, she would be beautiful and loved and that her beauty would make her mother and father better; universality: children experience varying degrees of self-blame when they sense problems between their parents and attempt to "fix" the problems by being more obedient and loving. pp. 44-46)*

4. Identify and discuss the three prostitutes who live above the Breedloves' storefront home, the symbolism of their names, and their importance to Pecola. *(China, Poland, and Miss Marie, a.k.a. the Maginot Line, are cheerful harridans who intrigue Pecola because they have many boyfriends. The women discuss why they became prostitutes. They hate men and do not respect women who deceive their husbands, but they do respect "good Christian colored women."; symbolism: Events in the novel take place in 1941, in the midst of World War II. Japan invaded China and China ultimately suffered over 2,000,000 casualties. Germany invaded Poland, the pawn in a non-aggression pact between Germany and Stalin, in 1939, beginning WWII. The Maginot Line, a fortified line of defense along the eastern border of France, was constructed after WWI. In 1940, the Germans invaded and captured the Maginot Line. Pecola finds refuge with the three women, and they treat her warmly. pp. 50-58)*

Supplementary Activities

1. Have students write a cinquain poem titled "Blue Eyes," reflecting Pecola's prayer for blue eyes. Pattern: Line 1: title; Line 2: two words to describe title; Line 3: three words to express

action about the title; Line 4: four words to express feeling about the title; Line 5: one word that is a synonym for the title.

2. As a class, write a diamente poem contrasting Redemption and Judgment. Refer to Mrs. Breedlove's interest in Christ the Judge rather than Christ the Redeemer (p. 42).

3. Have students research the allusion to Dillinger and the Lady in Red (p. 54). *(Anne Sage betrayed John Dillinger, one of the most notorious criminals in U.S. history, to federal agents. She told the agents she would be wearing a red dress.)*

4. Note the literary devices: **Similes**—a hated piece of furniture is like a sore tooth (p. 37); her (Mrs. Breedlove's) voice was like an earache in the brain (p. 41); the unquarreled evening hung like the first note of a dirge (p. 41); slowly, like Indian summer...he (Mr. Yacobowski) looks toward her (Pecola) (p. 48); his lumpy red hand plops around...like the agitated head of a chicken (p. 49); Poland's voice...sweet and hard like new strawberries (p. 51); laughter came like the sound of many rivers (p. 52) **Metaphors**—ugliness: mantle, shroud (p. 39); anger: puppy (p. 50) **Personification**—anger stirs and wakes in her (p. 50)

Winter

Pages 61–80 (first-person)

Pecola's self-esteem is further damaged through negative experiences with a group of boys and a new girl in school. Two of the prostitutes visit Mr. Henry at the MacTeers' home, where Claudia and Frieda meet them.

Vocabulary

gelid (61)	genuflected (62)	epiphany (63)	extemporized (65)
macabre (65)	mulatto (67)		

Discussion Questions

1. Examine the personification of Winter and the metaphors comparing Mr. MacTeer to winter. *(The coldness of the winter season is reflected in Mr. MacTeer's face. Eyes: cliff of snow, eyebrows: black limbs of leafless trees, skin: yellow of winter sun, jaw: snowbound field, forehead: frozen Lake Erie. He guards the family against the ravages of winter, keeping them safe from the "wolf" and "hawk" of cold and hunger. pp. 61-62)*

2. Analyze Pecola's harassment by the group of boys (how, why, effect). Correlate this with the "bully syndrome." *(The boys circle and hold at bay their "victim." Their taunts that she is black and that her father sleeps naked reflect their contempt of their own blackness and the similarities of their fathers with Pecola's; bully syndrome: the group's three-to-one majority gives them boldness and allows them to spew forth their own self-hatred and hopelessness against an innocent victim, relishing in Pecola's fear and embarrassment. The other girls confront them. The boys' brashness fades under the watchful gaze of Maureen and, rather than allow her to see them beat up the other girls, they pretend disinterest and leave. pp. 65-67)*

3. Characterize Maureen Peal and discuss her interaction with Pecola. *(She is a new student, a "high-yellow" child who has money and beautiful clothes. She captivates everyone in the school, white and black students as well as teachers. Claudia and Frieda are jealous of her but secretly would like to be her friend. She joins Claudia and Frieda in rescuing Pecola from a group of boys, and she initially befriends Pecola, curiously attempting to find out if the boys' taunts about her father are true. She gets into an argument with the three girls and begins to taunt Pecola, leaving her emotionally wounded. pp. 62-64, 67-73)*

4. Examine Claudia and Frieda's comparison of themselves with Maureen. Discuss the difference between jealousy and envy and the meaning of the "Thing" to fear. *(If Maureen, with her lighter skin and beautiful clothes is cute, Claudia and Frieda believe they are not. They see the admiration of adults and their peers when they look at Maureen, and believe that, even if they are nicer and brighter, they must be lesser than she. Although they have always been comfortable with themselves, Maureen arouses questions about their worthiness. They understand jealousy, the desire to have what someone else has, but envy, the desire to be someone else, is a new emotion for them; The "Thing" is whatever makes Maureen, but not them, beautiful—genealogy, money, or whatever they cannot change about themselves. p. 74)*

5. Discuss the MacTeer sisters' meeting with the prostitutes, how the girls reflect their mother's values, and why they decide not to tell her about the prostitutes. *(China and the Maginot Line are visiting Mr. Henry while the girls' parents are away. They recognize them as the women whom their mother hates and realize they should not be in the MacTeer home. Claudia believes China is not too bad, but she has heard terrible rumors about the Maginot Line and is unable to see or think anything good about her. Since Mrs. MacTeer vows she would never allow the Maginot Line to eat from one of her plates, the girls justify not telling their mother because the Maginot Line has not done so. pp. 77-79)*

Supplementary Activities

1. Have students create a montage that symbolizes Mr. MacTeer as "winter moves into his face."

2. As a class or individually, write a metaphor poem about Envy. Pattern—Line 1: noun; the subject; Lines 2-4: write something about the subject (each line should say something different and give an idea of what the subject is like); Line 5: a metaphor that begins with the title.

3. Elicit student response to the universality of Claudia and Frieda changing Maureen's name to "Meringue Pie" (p. 63). Ask for similar incidents students have encountered.

4. Note the literary devices: **Similes**—(group of boys) surround Pecola like a necklace of semiprecious stones (p. 65); legs look like wild dandelion stems; collars framing eyebrows like nuns' habits; angry faces knotted like dark cauliflowers; (Pecola) seemed to fold into herself like a pleated wing (p. 73) **Metaphors**—boys' anger: fiery cone of scorn; boys' actions: macabre ballet; Pecola: sacrificial victim (p. 65) **Allusions**—movie stars Betty Grable and Hedy Lamarr (p. 69); Greta Garbo and Ginger Rogers (p. 75); movie, "Imitation of Life," (1934) starring Claudette Colbert (p. 67)

Pages 81–93 (third-person)

Geraldine, the stereotype of a mannerly, moral, passionless, prejudiced black woman, and her son, Junior, add to Pecola's fear and heartache.

Vocabulary

inviolable (84)   surfeit (85)   ashen (87)   unabashed (92)

Discussion Questions

1. Analyze Geraldine and discuss her significance to the story. *(She is the stereotype of a southern black girl from a good neighborhood who is well-mannered, morally pure, thrifty, and passionless. She considers herself "colored," rather than black. She marries for respectability and a home, but is never able to give herself freely to her husband or to love her children although occasionally she will give her affection to an animal. She despises blacks who do not correspond with her standards. Geraldine moves to Lorain with her husband and they have one son, Louis, Jr. Her prejudice is obvious in her violent anger toward Pecola, in whom she sees every little black girl that she has despised all of her life. pp. 81-86, 91-92)*

2. Examine the importance of Geraldine and her relationship with Junior. *(She takes care of Junior physically but does not talk to him or show him affection. He becomes aware that she loves her cat more than she loves him, and he directs his hatred of his mother toward the cat. Geraldine insists that Junior play with white children, and she instills in him a hatred for other blacks. Although initially he wants to play with the black boys, he gradually comes to agree with his mother. He enjoys bullying girls, lies to his mother, and thinks the playground is his private territory. This sets the scene for his encounter with Pecola. pp. 86-88)*

3. Discuss Junior's cruelty toward Pecola, his mother's reaction, and the effect on Pecola. *(Junior challenges Pecola when she walks through his "yard," entices her to his house by promising to show her some kittens, and begins to harass her. Pecola is awed by the beautiful house but becomes frightened when he throws his mother's cat at her. He refuses to allow her to leave and shuts her up in a room but becomes enraged when she pets the cat. Symbolically, Pecola is enthralled with the blue eyes in the cat's black face. They struggle, and Junior throws the cat and kills it. His mother arrives, he blames Pecola for the cat's death, and Geraldine retaliates against her. As Pecola leaves, the coldness of the wind symbolizes the coldness in her heart. pp. 88-91)*

Supplementary Activities

1. Have students write a name poem about Pecola that describes her after she leaves Geraldine's house. Pattern: Place the letters of her name vertically on the paper. Write a descriptive word or phrase beginning with each letter.

2. Have students analyze the simile, "The light made them (the cat's eyes) shine like blue ice" (p. 90). *(Pecola is entranced by the cat's blue eyes in its black face, symbolizing her longing for blue eyes in her black face.)*

3. Note the similes—sound of Meridian opens windows of a room like first four notes of a hymn; girls like hollyhocks; Mobile girls are as sweet and plain as butter cake (pp. 81-82).

Spring

Pages 97–109 (first-person)

Mr. Henry makes sexual advances toward Frieda. The MacTeer sisters visit Pecola at her mother's place of employment. Mrs. Breedlove reacts violently toward Pecola, yet she treats the Fisher's child with tenderness and love.

Vocabulary
shards (104)

Discussion Questions

1. Analyze the incident between Mr. Henry and Frieda. Note the reactions of Frieda, Mr. and Mrs. MacTeer, Miss Dunion, and Claudia and what they typify. *(Mr. Henry fondles Frieda's breasts. She tells her mother, who tells her father, and together the parents attack him, forcing Mr. Henry to run away. This signifies Frieda's trust in her parents and her parents' belief in and protectiveness toward their children. Frieda, symbolizing family loyalty, hits Rosemary for implying that Mr. MacTeer is going to jail. Miss Dunion, who mentions that Frieda might by "ruined," typifies the nosy neighbor who makes everyone's business her own, causing Frieda to fear becoming fat like the "ruined" prostitute. Claudia depicts the child's point of view with her solution. p. 97-101)*

2. Discuss the MacTeer girls' visit to the Fisher home. Elicit student response to the significance of Mrs. Breedlove's reaction to Pecola and to the Fisher child. *(Frieda and Claudia are enthralled with the beauty of the lakefront homes and the park, which black people are not allowed to enter, showing the contrast between their world and the white people's world. Pecola is outside the house waiting for her mother to bring the laundry. The three girls step inside the kitchen, and Pecola accidentally knocks a berry cobbler to the floor. Her mother, oblivious to Pecola's burns, knocks her to the floor and screams at her to get out. In contrast, she consoles the Fishers' blonde, beautiful little girl, speaking softly and lovingly to her. This further imbeds feelings of ugliness and self-hatred into Pecola's heart. pp. 105-109)*

Supplementary Activities

1. Note the universality of Claudia's statement, "I just get tired of having everything last" (p. 100). Have students complete the statement, "I just get tired...", relating it to their feelings about adolescence.

2. Have students draw a caricature of Miss Marie based on the metaphors and similes relating to her. Maginot Line: mountain of flesh; massive legs like tree stumps; two roads of soft flabby inner thigh that kissed each other deep in the shade of her dress and closed; a dark-brown bottle growing out of her dimpled hand like a burned limb; eyes clear as rain; eyes: waterfall (pp. 102-103).

Pages 110–131 (third-person omniscient)

Note the stream-of-consciousness scattered throughout this section.

The reader learns about Pauline (Williams) Breedlove's background. She attributes the death of her dreams to her lame foot and her loss of a front tooth. She and Cholly love each other when they marry, but the marriage deteriorates into quarrels and fights, with only occasional flashbacks to the good times. She plants seeds of rejection in her children.

Vocabulary
infirmity (116)   coherence (126)   virtues (128)   slovenliness (129)

Discussion Questions

1. Examine Pauline (Williams) Breedlove's background and analyze how it shapes her future. *(A childhood injury leaves her with a lame foot to which she attributes the death of her dreams. She feels isolated from others and takes refuge in neatly arranging "things." Her family migrates to Kentucky, where Pauline cares for her younger siblings. She dreams of a "Presence," a Stranger who will take her away from her monotonous life. When Cholly Breedlove appears, she believes that he is her Stranger. They fall in love, marry, and move up north. After the birth of her children and the disintegration of her marriage, Pauline finds fulfillment in keeping the Fishers' home and caring for their child. The Fishers appreciate her, and in their home she can keep beautiful things neatly in order. pp. 110-117, 126-128)*

2. Discuss the disintegration of the Breedloves' marriage. Correlate with the universal effects of loneliness, dissatisfaction, dependency, and fantasy on a marriage. *(After they move north, Pauline becomes lonely and dependent on Cholly for all her emotional needs. She doesn't fit in with the other black women and feels inadequate around them. Cholly's consideration of her wanes. They begin to focus on money because of her desire for clothes and his desire for liquor, and their quarrels escalate into fights. Pauline becomes pregnant and takes refuge in movies, fantasizing about her own physical beauty, the perfect man, and the perfect marriage. Her fantasies make her feel uglier and make Cholly increasingly undesirable to her. She eventually takes on the responsibility of breadwinner for the family and becomes religious, viewing Cholly as the model of sin; universality: the same pressures and fantasies destroy marriages today. pp. 117-126)*

3. Discuss Pauline's view of marriage and motherhood and her reaction to Pecola. Ask students how they think Pecola's mother's reaction to her affects Pecola's self-image. *(Neither marriage nor motherhood is what Pauline expects. Her idealized dream turns into worry, and she takes her frustrations out on the children, screaming at them and beating them. Pecola is not the dream child Pauline envisions. She thinks Pecola is smart but ugly. Pecola grows up believing she is ugly and suffers from very low self-esteem. pp. 123-126)*

4. Examine the effect Pauline's employment has on her and on her children. *(The beauty and orderliness of the Fishers' home, the abundance of food, and the loveliness of the little blonde-headed child cause Pauline to view her own home and family unfavorably. She feels a sense of her own worth in her job. She begins to neglect her house, her husband, and her children and teaches*

them fear of being clumsy, being like their father, not being loved by God, and of madness like Cholly's mother. Sammy reacts with the desire to run away, and Pecola reacts by fearing life. pp. 126-128)

Supplementary Activities
1. Have students write a metaphor poem about Fear based on the fear Pauline instills in her children (p. 128). Pattern—Line 1: noun (subject); Lines 2-4: write something about the subject (each line should say something different and give an idea of what the subject is like); Line 5: a metaphor that begins with the title.

2. Have students analyze the metaphor that compares Pauline's isolation to the "cocoon of her family's spinning" (p. 111).

3. Have students analyze the simile, "Holding Cholly as a model of sin and failure, she bore him like a crown of thorns, and her children like a cross" (pp. 126-127).

4. Note the other literary devices: **Similes**—she (the baby) looked like a black ball of hair (p. 124); muscles like peach stones (p. 129) **Metaphors**—Lorain, Ohio: melting pot on the lip of America (p. 117); children's hair: tangled black puffs of rough wool (p. 127)

Pages 132–163 (third-person omniscient)

The reader learns about Cholly's background. Abandoned by his mother when he was four days old, his great aunt raises him. After her death, his search for his father ends in rejection. Marriage and fatherhood drive him to despair, culminating in his rape of Pecola.

Vocabulary

prolific (136)	infallibility (137)	furtive (138)	shrouded (139)
synthesized (139)	fastidious (140)	omnipresence (143)	dysfunctional (160)

Discussion Questions
1. Examine Cholly's background: his birth and abandonment, his "adoption" by Great Aunt Jimmy, the importance of Blue Jack, and his humiliation by the white men. Analyze the effect of his background on his role as husband and father. *(His mother abandons him four days after his birth, his father leaves before he is born, and his great aunt rescues, loves, and raises him but dies when he is thirteen years old. Cholly loves elderly Blue Jack, who becomes a temporary father figure to him. White men humiliate him when they catch him and Darlene in a sexual encounter, causing him to turn his anger toward her and run away to find his father, who rejects him. The loss of everyone in his life, his lack of stability, and his low self-esteem leave him "free" to come and go and to treat others as he pleases. He drinks to escape the monotony of marriage and fatherhood. pp. 132-161)*

2. Discuss Great Aunt Jimmy's illness and death. Discuss her treatment by M'Dear and others. Note the term "slop jar" and elicit student response. *(Great Aunt Jimmy becomes ill from being damp and cold. Treatment includes camomile tea, liniment, and Bible reading. M'Dear orders them to bury the slop jar with its contents and for Great Aunt Jimmy to drink only pot liquor. She eats some peach cobbler, and the women attribute her death to that. pp. 135-140)*

3. Discuss the recitation of their "life cycle" by the black women and ask students whether or not they think this is a true representation of black women of the early 20th century. *(The laughter of youth turns to the trials of young women. They have to take orders from everyone except black children and each other. They care for the homes of white women. White men beat their husbands, the women clean up the blood, and their men beat them in frustration and retaliation. The paradox of their lives includes beating their children, yet stealing for them; strength to cut down trees, butcher hogs, wring the necks of chickens and plow the fields, yet gentleness to cut umbilical cords, nurture African violets, rock babies to sleep, and make love to their husbands. The cycle ends in old age, where they are free from the responsibilities of raising children and from the fear of the cruelty of others. pp. 137-139)*

4. Analyze Cholly's hatred of Darlene, based on the statement, "For now, he hated the one who had created the situation, the one who bore witness to his failure, his impotence" (p. 151). Ask students if they think his reaction is typical of human nature. *(To hate the white men will destroy him because they are big, white, and armed, and he is small, black, and helpless. Therefore, he turns his hatred toward Darlene because he hates himself for being unable to protect her, and she knows his weaknesses.)*

5. Analyze the situation that leads Cholly to rape Pecola and whether or not he intends to do it. *(He is drunk when he sees her in the kitchen. He feels revulsion, guilt, and pity for her because she looks so vulnerable and unhappy. He has nothing to give her and there is nothing he can do for her. Yet, he knows she loves him. Her scratching the back of her calf with her toe triggers memories of Pauline and he begins to feel tender, protective lust toward Pecola. Confused with memories of Pauline and the excitement of doing a forbidden thing, he rapes Pecola. Conflicting emotions of hate and tenderness fill him and he covers her with a quilt. pp. 161-163)*

Supplementary Activities

1. Read aloud the Emancipation Proclamation and discuss its after-effects. Compare with the memories of the black women.

2. Note the literary devices: **Similes**—M'Dear standing straight as a poker (p. 136); turn of their necks like a doe's (p. 138); they came home to nestle like plums under the limbs of their men (p. 138); it (the funeral) was like a street tragedy (p. 143); they (Darlene's hands) looked like baby claws (p. 148); vacancy in his head like space left by newly pulled tooth (p. 150); hating them would have...burned him up like a piece of soft coal (p. 151); no more thought than a chick leaving its shell (p. 152); minutes of those hours struggled like gnats on fly paper (p. 153); men clustered like grapes; rubbing the dice as though they were two hot coals (p. 154); sunshine dropped like honey on his head (p. 156); the dark...enclosed Cholly like skin and flesh of an elderberry protecting its own seed (p. 157); hollow suck of air...like rapid loss of air from a circus balloon (p. 163) **Metaphors**—heart of the watermelon: nasty, sweet guts of the earth (p. 135); funeral banquet: pearl of joy (p. 142); quarrels: sticking gravy on everybody's tongue (p. 151)

Pages 164–183 (third-person omniscient)

Soaphead Church, a.k.a. Elihue Micah Whitcomb, is introduced. He is a self-appointed psychic and is a pedophile. Pecola, pregnant with Cholly's child, comes to him to ask him to give her blue eyes.

Vocabulary

misanthrope (164)	antipathies (164)	asceticism (165)	celibacy (165)
diffident (166)	parody (167)	Anglophilia (168)	eccentricity (168)
predilection (169)	avocation (170)	poignant (174)	imbibed (182)

Discussion Questions

1. Identify Soaphead Church and examine his idiosyncrasies. *(He is a West Indian by birth, his grandfather was a religious fanatic and his father a violent schoolmaster who instilled in his son fear and self-deception. His mother died soon after his birth. Soaphead's wife left him two months after their marriage because of his fastidious, melancholy nature and he has never recovered. After failing as a minister, he proclaims himself to be a spiritualist and psychic reader, counseling those who are shrouded with anger, loneliness, misery, etc. He prefers the collection of old objects to human contact with the exception of his occasional pedophiliac cravings, preying on little girls who come to him. He rents a room from Bertha Reese and hates her old dog, Bob. pp. 164-171)*

2. Analyze why Soaphead calls Velma his "Beatrice." Note the reference to Soaphead's love of Dante's work and compare/contrast Dante's love for Beatrice with Soaphead's love for Velma. *(Beatrice was the great love of Dante's life; Velma is the great love of Soaphead's life. Dante first met Beatrice when he was nine years old; Soaphead meets Velma when he is a teenager. Beatrice married someone else and died young; Velma marries Soaphead but leaves him after two months. Dante never forgot Beatrice, and she remained a strong influence in his life. She figures prominently in many of his works; e.g., "Vita Nuova" and each section of* The Divine Comedy, *where she appears as a symbol of divine love; Soaphead never forgets Velma, and his grief for her figures prominently in his letter to God. She remains a strong influence in his life. pp. 169-170)*

3. Examine Pecola's request of Soaphead and his response. *(She is now pregnant with Cholly's child, has had to drop out of school, and asks Soaphead to give her blue eyes. He feels mixed emotions toward her—love, understanding, and anger—and wishes he could work a miracle for her. He manipulates her into believing that she will receive the blue eyes if she makes "contact with nature" by feeding Bob. He tells her that if the old dog behaves strangely, she will know God has granted her request. In reality, he gives her poisoned meat and Bob dies, but Pecola takes this as a sign that she has received her blue eyes. pp. 173-176)*

4. Analyze Soaphead's letter to God. *(The letter summarizes all of his complaints about God and identifies his [Soaphead's] real persona. He reveals the following: the inhabitants of his West Indian colony took on the worst characteristics of their white masters; he grieves for Velma, his wife; he is enthralled with the bodies of little girls, especially their breasts; he admits that he lives a lie but justifies his lifestyle because of God's failure. He believes he has had to do God's work for Him because God has neglected Pecola and failed to answer her prayers for blue eyes. He tells God that Pecola will have blue eyes that only she will see. pp. 176-182)*

Supplementary Activities

1. Have students write a limerick about Soaphead Church.

2. Assign the following allusions to individuals and have them report to the class: Hamlet's abuse of Ophelia, Christ's love of Mary Magdalene, Othello's love for Desdemona, Iago's perverted love of Othello, references to Dante and Dostoyevsky (p. 169). Students should correlate these with Soaphead's view of love.

3. Note the literary devices: **Metaphors**—celibacy: haven; silence: shield (p. 165); little girls breasts: buds; little girls: saplings (179); Elihue's mind: soundless cave (170) **Biblical Allusions**—"Suffer the little children to come unto me, and harm them not" (p. 181): Matthew 19:14

Spring, Afterword

Pages 187–216

Claudia summarizes the reactions and events following Pecola's rape. Pecola slips into a world of her own, where she and her hallucinatory friend discuss the beauty of Pecola's blue eyes. In the afterword, Toni Morrison reveals that she based *The Bluest Eye* on a black elementary school student's wish for blue eyes and Morrison's reaction to the child's racial self-hatred.

Vocabulary

holocaust (187)	*Moirai* (188)	devious (191)	tendril (204)
inarticulateness (205)	eloquent (205)	honed (205)	matrix (206)
volition (206)	acquiesce (206)		

Discussion Questions

1. Examine the gossip relating to Pecola's pregnancy. Note the commonality of blaming the girl. *(The general consensus is that Cholly is crazy, Pecola is foolish, and that they should remove her from school because she carries some of the blame. The talk reveals that Cholly has left, Mrs. Breedlove beat Pecola after the rape, no one believes the baby will live, and it is bound to be ugly if it does. Claudia and Frieda are the only ones who feel sorry for Pecola and want the baby to live. pp. 166-190)*

2. Discuss Claudia and Frieda's attempt to "make a miracle," analyze the rationale of the girls, and discuss the result of their bargain. *(They have been selling marigold seeds to make money to buy a bicycle. They attempt to bargain with God: they will be good for a month and will give up their plans for a bicycle by burying the money they have made and plant the marigold seeds if Pecola's baby is allowed to live. They rationalize that, if the seeds sprout, they will know everything is all right; result: Pecola's baby dies, driving her into madness. Claudia and Frieda avoid Pecola because they blame themselves for failing Pecola and her baby. pp. 191-192, 204-206)*

3. Have two students read Pecola's "conversation" aloud. Note the stream-of-consciousness and analyze the content. *(Through stream-of-consciousness, Pecola reveals the following: her mother will never look directly at her, people ignore her, Pecola is no longer allowed to attend school, she never talks to anyone but her imaginary friend, she has observed her parents' sexual encounters, she is in denial that the rape actually occurred, Cholly attempted to rape her again [possibly succeeded], her mother refused to believe Pecola when she told her about the rape, and Cholly and Sammy are both gone. Pecola believes her eyes are blue but fears they are not the bluest. pp. 193-204)*

4. Discuss Pecola's life after the rape and death of her baby. *(She spends her days talking to her hallucinatory friend, staying alone in her little house or walking up and down, flailing her arms as if attempting to fly, and searching the garbage. pp. 204-206)*

5. Analyze why Morrison wrote *The Bluest Eye* and whether or not she feels she has achieved her objective. *(She based the story on the wish of a black elementary student to have blue eyes. She explores the depth of racial self-hatred and the destruction of a little black girl. Morrison believes it has taken twenty-five years to gain respect for the novel and, symbolically, for Pecola. pp. 209-216)*

Supplementary Activities

1. Have students list the symptoms and research the type of Pecola's mental illness.

2. As a class, write name poems for Claudia and Frieda.

3. Have students write a critique for the novel.

Post-reading Discussion Questions

1. Diagram the cycle of rejection by placing three circles on the overhead transparency, two side by side with arrows joining them to one below. Place Cholly, Pauline, and Pecola's names in the three circles. Brainstorm with students about rejection and its results. For example, in the first circle, list Cholly's abandonment by his mother, his rejection by his father, his humiliation by the white men, his drinking, his inability to keep a job, and his rejection by Pauline. In the second circle, list Pauline's birth, the injury causing her lame foot, her mistreatment by her first employer, her disappointment in marriage and motherhood, and her mistreatment of her children. Place Pecola's name in the third circle and list the results of her rejection.

2. Refer to headings using excerpts from the Dick and Jane reading primer at the beginning of the third-person omniscient sections. Discuss why the lines begin to run together. Note how the headings, describing a "perfect" white family correlate with the tragic developments in Pecola's family and Pecola's life.

3. Analyze the effectiveness of the first-person narrative by Pecola's friend and why the author switches back and forth between first-person and third-person omniscient, including the use of stream-of-consciousness. *(Claudia gives a personal insight into her friend's plight. The third-person sections reveal facts about the family and events that Claudia would not have known about. Stream-of-consciousness segments reveal personal insight into events.)*

4. Analyze the effectiveness of the title. Ask students if they can think of a more appropriate title. If so, why?

5. Analyze the evidence of racial self-hatred in the novel and how it destroys the lives of some of the characters. Include an analysis of racism: white/black; mulatto/black; affluent black/poor. *(Pecola's intense longing for blue eyes so she will be "beautiful" and "loved"; Cholly's humiliation by the white men and his ensuing feelings of self-hatred; Pauline Breedlove's love for the "white" world of the Fishers and her neglect of her own children and home while devoting herself to the Fishers' beautiful home and child; Maureen Peal's need to be the "cutest" because even her beautiful clothes and money can't eliminate the fact that she is half black; Geraldine's hatred of most other blacks, her wish to keep her world like that of the white women, and her manipulation of her son to hate blacks; Soaphead Church's ancestors' desire to marry those whiter than themselves so they appear more white than black.)*

6. Analyze the character of Cholly Breedlove. *(The author condemns his actions, especially the raping of Pecola, yet she attributes his self-hatred and his actions to his own rejection as a child and his humiliation by the white men.)*

7. Trace the pattern of Pecola's rejection. *(Her mother instills "ugliness" in her; her father ignores her, fails to provide for her, and ultimately rapes her; the teachers and children at school act as if she isn't there or use her as the scapegoat for cruelty; the group of boys taunt her about her color and her father; Maureen Peal's "friendship" turns to cruelty, Mr. Yacobowski treats her with contempt; Geraldine and Junior treat her maliciously, Soaphead Church manipulates her; public opinion blames her in part for the rape.)*

8. Analyze the importance of genealogy in the novel. *(Cholly's mother abandons him, his father rejects him; he, in turn, neglects his own children. Pauline's lame foot causes her shame, the black women up north make her embarrassed and ashamed, and she longs for the white standard of beauty. She, in turn, pronounces Pecola ugly from the time of her birth, causing Pecola to feel ugly, rejected, and inadequate. The entire Breedlove family faces the world with the "mantle of ugliness" [p. 39]. The men of Soaphead Church's family were corrupt and lecherous; his grandfather was a religious fanatic and his father was violent; Soaphead reflects these familial characteristics. pp. 167-169)*

9. Analyze the symbolism of nature in the novel. *(The novel is segmented into events in the Autumn, Winter, Spring, and Summer. One interpretation—Autumn: the Breedlove family "reaps the harvest" of rejection, anger, poverty, and racism from "seeds" that are referred to the Spring section. Winter: "seeds" of hatred that have lain dormant in Geraldine culminate in further destruction of Pecola. Spring: the "seeds" of Pauline and Cholly's lives produce Pecola's total destruction. Other references to nature include the comparison between the marigold seeds that do not grow in the earth and Cholly's seed which does not grow properly in Pecola, and Pecola's love for dandelions, which turns to hate after Mr. Yacobowski's contempt. Claudia summarizes the hostility of the land in her reference to the bad soil and her analogy between the marigold seeds and Pecola, "This soil is bad for certain kinds of flowers. Certain seeds it will not nurture, certain fruit it will not bear, and when the land kills of its own volition, we acquiesce and say the victim had no right to live." [p. 206])*

10. Discuss the symbolism of the three prostitutes and relate to historical events of the early 1940s. (See information in second discussion question section of this guide.)

11. Refer to the two lists relating to a child's self-esteem in the Initiating Activities section of this guide. Discuss with students both the positive and negative influences that mold Pecola.

Post-reading Extension Activities

Writing
1. Write and perform a song about Cholly Breedlove.

2. Write a series of Public Service Announcements directed toward parents. These can be one-minute ads for radio or television or one-line ads for newspapers. Include suggestions for instilling self-esteem in children.

3. Write and illustrate a children's story based on Pecola's experience with Maureen Peal.

4. Write a lament telling the story of Pecola.

5. Write a diamente poem contrasting Self-esteem and Self-degradation.

Art
1. Create a collage depicting Rejection and Self-hatred.

2. Select and bring to class pictures showing children of a variety of races/ethnicities. Write a caption referring to the beauty in each child.

Drama/Music
1. Write a TV script for one of the scenes from the novel. Select and play appropriate background music as you stage the scene.

2. Write and perform a ballad about Pecola.

Current Events
1. Select and bring to class articles that relate to the abuse of children.

2. Select and bring to class articles that relate to anorexia or bulimia. Present an oral discussion of these two types of self-hatred and correlate with Pecola's self-hatred.

Language Study
Prepare a class dictionary that identifies examples of dialect in the novel.

Other Reading
Read Maya Angelou's novel, *I Know Why the Caged Bird Sings*. Give an oral report to the class, comparing Ms. Angelou and Pecola Breedlove.

Assessment for *The Bluest Eye*

Assessment is an ongoing process. The following ten items can be completed during the novel study. Once finished, the student and teacher will check the work. Points may be added to indicate the level of understanding.

Name _____ Date _____

Student   **Teacher**

_____   _____   1. Correct all quizzes and worksheets for review.

_____   _____   2. Write a critique of the novel.

_____   _____   3. Display or perform your extension projects on the assigned day.

_____   _____   4. Write a one-word response as the teacher calls out the names of various characters.

_____   _____   5. Write a review question over each of the four sections of the novel. Participate in an oral review.

_____   _____   6. Provide examples from the novel that show the decline of Pecola Breedlove.

_____   _____   7. Compare your completed character charts, story maps, and comprehension activities in small groups of three or four.

_____   _____   8. Write a bio-poem for Pecola. Pattern—Line 1: name; Line 2: four of her traits; Line 3: designation (daughter, sister...); Line 4: feels...; Line 5: needs...; Line 6: gives...; Line 7: fears...; Line 8: regrets...; Line 9: destiny (in the book).

_____   _____   9. Write a two-line description of one of the characters but omit the name. Exchange with a partner and identify the character (s)he has described.

_____   _____   10. Identify how the novel reflects the following types of conflict: person against person and person against himself/herself. Use specific examples from the novel.

© Novel Units, Inc.   All rights reserved

Glossary

Preface-page 32

1. melancholy (preface): low spirits; sadness

2. senile (14): showing weakness often characterized by old age

3. peripheral (17): having to do with, situated in, or forming an outside boundary

4. plaintive (21): sad, mournful

5. acridness (22): sharpness, bitterness

6. pristine (23): original, primitive; in the earliest stage

7. sadism (23): pleasure experienced from infliction of pain on others; delight in cruelty or pain

8. soliloquies (24): speeches to oneself

9. chagrined (24): disappointed; feeling failure or humiliation

10. verification (31): proof by evidence or testimony

Pages 33-58

1. foists (33): to pass off as genuine, valuable, or worthy; imposes by fraud

2. furtiveness (36): stealthily doing something to avoid being noticed; secretiveness

3. malaise (37): a vague feeling of bodily discomfort or disturbance

4. dissipation (38): a wasting by misuse; indulgence in sensual or foolish pleasures

5. emasculations (42): acts that destroy, weaken, or deprive virility

6. tacitly (43): implied or understood without being openly expressed; implicitly, naturally

7. inexplicable (50): that which cannot be explained, understood, or accounted for; mysterious

8. petulant (50): unreasonably ill-tempered; irritable, peevish, overly trifling

9. epithets (51): descriptive expressions; words or phrases expressing some quality or attribute

10. covert (56): secret, hidden, disguised

Pages 61-93

1. gelid (61): cold as ice; frosty, frozen

2. genuflected (62): bending the knee as an act of reverence or worship

3. epiphany (63): a sudden revelation or perception; insight

4. extemporized (65): spoken or composed as one goes along; improvised

5. macabre (65): causing horror; gruesome, ghastly

6. mulatto (67): a person of mixed white and black descent

7. inviolable (84): that which must not be violated or injured; sacred

8. surfeit (85): an excessive amount of something; excess

9. ashen (87): the color of ashes; pale

10. unabashed (92): not embarrassed, ashamed, or awed; bold

Pages 97-131

1. shards (104): broken pieces; fragments

2. infirmity (116): weakness, feebleness

3. coherence (126): logical connections; consistency, congruity

4. virtues (128): good qualities; merits

5. slovenliness (129): lack of neatness; dirtiness; carelessness in appearance, dress, habits, or work

Pages 132-163

1. prolific (136): producing much

2. infallibility (137): absolute freedom from error; inability to be mistaken

3. furtive (138): secretive, sly, stealthy, shifty

4. shrouded (139): covered, concealed, veiled

5. synthesized (139): put together or combined into a complex whole

6. fastidious (140): excessively discriminatory; exacting; displaying meticulous attention to detail

7. omnipresence (143): present everywhere at the same time

8. dysfunctional [alternate spelling–disfunctional] (160): performing badly or improperly; malfunctioning

Pages 164-183

1. misanthrope (164): a person who dislikes or distrusts people in general; hater of humanity

2. antipathies (164): strong or fixed dislikes; aversions; feelings against

3. asceticism (165): unusual or extreme self-denial and self-discipline

4. celibacy (165): abstinence in sexual matters

5. diffident (166): lacking in self-confidence; shy, bashful

6. parody (167): humorous exaggerated imitation of a literary work, style, author, etc.

7. Anglophilia (168): a devotion to England, its culture, or its people

8. eccentricity (168): something out of the ordinary; oddity, peculiarity

9. predilection (169): a liking; preference

10. avocation (170): a calling or vocation

11. poignant (174): very painful; piercing; moving or touching

12. imbibed (182): to drink in; to absorb

Pages 187–216

1. holocaust (187): great or wholesale destruction

2. *Moirai* (188): any one of the three Fates; a person's fate or kind of life decreed by the Fates

3. devious (191): straying from the right course; not straightforward; underhanded

4. tendril (204): twisting, threadlike strand that attaches itself to something

5. inarticulateness (205): not distinct; not uttered in distinct syllables or words

6. eloquent (205): fluent and expressive use of language

7. honed (205): sharpened

8. matrix (206): center; womb; mold for casting

9. volition (206): act of willing decision or choice

10. acquiesce (206): to give consent; to accept by keeping silent or by not making objections